The ultimate bu[...]
from Bloom[...]

The new *Business Essentials* series [...] handy
pocket guides on a wide range of b[...] writing a CV and
performing well in interviews, to ma[...]ost impactful presentations,
finding the right work/life balance, brushing up your business writing skills,
managing projects effectively, and becoming more assertive at work.

Writing Skills for Business
How to communicate clearly to get your message across

Manage Projects Successfully
How to make things happen on time and on budget

Assert Yourself
How to find your voice and make your mark

Succeed as a New Manager
How to inspire your team and be a great boss

Balance your Life and Work
How to get the best from your job and still have a Life

Give Great Presentations
How to speak confidently and make your point

Get that Job: Interviews
How to keep your head and land your ideal job

Deal With Stress
Improving your health through changing how you work

Get that Job: CVs and Resumes
How to make sure you stand out from the crowd

**Available from all good retailers and bookshops,
as well as from Bloomsbury.com**

BLOOMSBURY BUSINESS

Get That Job: Interviews

How to keep your head and get your ideal job

BLOOMSBURY BUSINESS
LONDON · OXFORD · NEW YORK · NEW DELHI · SYDNEY

BLOOMSBURY BUSINESS
Bloomsbury Publishing Plc
50 Bedford Square, London, WC1B 3DP, UK
29 Earlsfort Terrace, Dublin 2, Ireland

BLOOMSBURY, BLOOMSBURY BUSINESS and the Diana logo are trademarks
of Bloomsbury Publishing Plc

First published in Great Britain in 2004 by Bloomsbury Publishing Plc
Revised edition published in 2009 by Bloomsbury Publishing Plc
(under the A&C Black imprint)
This revised and updated edition published in 2022 by
Bloomsbury Publishing Plc

A catalogue record for this book is available from the British Library

Library of Congress Cataloguing-in-Publication data has been applied for

ISBN: 978-1-4729-9329-8; eBook: 978-1-4729-9330-4

2 4 6 8 10 9 7 5 3 1

Text design by seagulls.net

Typeset by Deanta Global Publishing Services, Chennai, India
Printed and bound in Great Britain by CPI Group (UK) Ltd, Croydon CR0 4YY

To find out more about our authors and books visit www.bloomsbury.com
and sign up for our newsletters

Contents

Assess yourself: How good are your interview skills?

It is important to be well prepared for your interview so you don't get caught out by an unexpected or tricky question. By answering these questions carefully and honestly you will be making a positive step towards interview success. The questions should help you start developing your case for why you are indeed the best candidate for the job. It is a good idea to read Chapter 1 before answering the questions below.

In questions where you are asked to give a rating, 1 is the lowest grade (i.e. poor, very little) and 5 the highest (i.e. excellent, very much).

1. Give yourself a rating that reflects how comfortable you feel in interviews.

    1   2   3   4   5

(If you are at the lower end of the scale then careful planning should help you gain in confidence and market yourself better. Think carefully about these questions and the extra questions in Chapter 1, writing down longer answers at first then condensing them into more concise explanations. Read Chapter 3 so you are prepared to deal with the situation if you are asked inappropriate questions.)

2. What is it about the organization that has made you apply for the position?

(If you are struggling to answer this question, spend some more time researching the organization that has invited you for interview. See Chapter 1.)

3. Be honest! To what extent is your interest in your chosen job genuine and to what extent is it attractive because of its high profile, good salary etc.?

    1   2   3   4   5

4. Give three reasons why you want this job. (It is important to be aware of your own motives so you can be prepared for tricky questions.)

5. Is there anything you would like to know about the organization and/or position, to help you decide whether the job will suit you? (The interviewer will almost always ask you whether you have any questions, so it is important to have a few well-thought-out queries. See Chapter 1 for ideas.)

6. Is there anything you have glossed over or left out of your CV (for example, lots of job changes, leaving school/college/university early, a long period of unemployment)? You are likely to be asked about this – how can you explain it? (For advice on dealing with tricky questions, read Chapter 2. The list in this chapter gives examples of potentially challenging areas of questioning that you should be prepared for.)

7. Name three of your weaknesses. How might you overcome them? (This is a popular interview question so it's important to have an answer ready!)

8. What are your three main strengths? Are you able to back up each of these strengths? Why have you chosen them?

9. How would you rate your career experience to date?

   1   2   3   4   5

10. Describe your most formative experience.

11. Rate the experience gained from your spare-time activities and travel.

    1   2   3   4   5

12. Which is your most important interest outside of work and why? Can you apply your experience/ interests positively to what is wanted by your potential employer?

13. Think of good examples to show how you have developed each of the following competences:

   - planning and organizing
   - decision-making
   - communicating
   - influencing others
   - teamwork
   - achieving results
   - leadership
   - diplomacy

(Competence-related questions are becoming more and more common. Build on these answers so you are prepared. For hints on how to do this, see Chapter 6.)

1
Making an impact in interviews

Congratulations! You've cleared the first hurdle in your job search with a great CV and covering letter, and have been invited for an interview – you've already found some way to stand out from the crowd. Now you need to build on this success. As you prepare yourself mentally and emotionally for your interview, keep these questions in mind:

- Why do you think you are the best person for the job?

- What is it about this job that attracts you?

- What is it about this organization that has made you apply for the position?

- Who will interview you and what do you know about them?

- What is the appropriate dress and/or image for this organization?

Step one:
Do your homework

Review your CV or application form

✔ Remind yourself thoroughly of all the information on your CV or application form. Think about what questions you might be asked based on your education or work history.

Questions that might be difficult to answer include, 'Why did you choose to study this subject?', 'Why did you leave your last job?' or 'Why did you have a period of unemployment?' Write notes about what you are going to say and practise your answers.

Research the organization

Finding out as much as you can about the company you are visiting will not only help you decide if it is the sort of organization you would like to work for, but may also give you some ideas for questions to ask the interviewer. If you find an opportunity to show that you have done your research, this will signal to the interviewer that you are enthusiastic about the job, as well as knowledgeable about the market.

✔ Look at the company's website and social media feeds, focusing on the annual report, news, press releases and biographies. This will give you a feel for the organization – its key values, its success factor and its people.

✔ Research current factors that might affect the organization, such as industry trends, competitive issues, strategic direction and particular challenges or opportunities.

Step two:
Decide what you want to get from the interview

✓ Identify the key points you want to make about your strengths and skills. When you prepared your CV, you listed the key strengths and skills that you thought an employer would be looking for. Re-visit that list, choose a skill and think of a recent situation you have been in that will demonstrate that strength or skill to an interviewer. If possible, include any concrete results achieved due to that particular strength or skill.

TOP TIP

It is important to focus on the positive in your answers, even when you have been asked to talk about a difficult situation or your weaknesses. That way, you will come across as someone who rises to a challenge and looks for opportunities to improve and develop.

✓ Prepare a mental list of questions you would like to ask the interviewer(s). Remember that you are also interviewing the organization, so put together a list of questions that will help you decide whether or not this job is a good fit for your personality and your career goals. In addition, well-thought-out and pertinent questions will help to demonstrate your interest in the company and your enthusiasm for the post.

> **TOP TIP**
>
> Avoid asking questions about benefits and salary at a first interview, unless the interviewer brings them up. Get the offer first, then talk about money! For advice on negotiating a good benefits package, see Chapter 14.

Step three:
Prepare yourself mentally

Many people, from athletes to salespeople, prepare themselves for challenging situations by mentally picturing a successful result – a method that can also be used before attending an interview.

✔ Before the interview, imagine yourself being professional, interesting and enthusiastic in your interview. Also imagine yourself leaving the interview with a good feeling about how you did. This will put you in a positive frame of mind and help you to be at your very best in the interview.

✔ Arrive 15 or 20 minutes early so that you can take some time to relax after your journey. Go and freshen up to help you feel more comfortable and confident. Drink some water, flick through company magazines if they are available. Try to get a feel for the atmosphere, as this will help you to decide if it's the sort of place you can see yourself being happy working in. It will also give you an idea of what to expect in the interview and the sort of candidate the interviewers will be looking for.

✔ Ask a friend or family member to role-play the interview with you. School and university career counsellors and career coaches will also do this. Give this person a list of questions that you think you might be asked. Role-play the interview and ask for the other person's feedback. Film it if you can so that you can watch your body language.

Typical interview questions

Prepare answers to these standard questions that interviewers often ask:

- Tell me a little bit about yourself.
- Where do you see your career five years from now?
- What are you most proud of in your career?
- What is your greatest strength?
- What is your biggest weakness?
- Describe a difficult situation and how you handled it.
- Can you tell me about a time when you had to motivate a team?

If you are a recent graduate, be prepared to answer questions like these:

- Why did you choose your degree subject?
- How will your studies relate to your work?
- What have you enjoyed most at university?

TOP TIP

When asked to tell the interviewer a bit about yourself, they don't want a life history. The interviewer is using this as an ice-breaker so give a brief overview of yourself, including a short history of recent employment.

Step four:
Create a positive impression during the interview

✓ Be punctual. Better still, be early to give yourself some preparation and relaxation time. If you're not sure of the location of the company, you might want to do a practice run of the journey so you can be sure to leave yourself enough time.

✓ Be enthusiastic. Know why you are interested in this job and make sure you show your interest. Interviewees who are excited about the organization get job offers! Don't say that you are interested in the job because it pays well. Instead, be ready to talk about what you can offer the company, how the position will expand your skills and why this kind of work would be satisfying and meaningful to you. Don't overdo it, though, as this may come across as insincere or overconfident.

✓ Be honest. The overall impression you are trying to create is of an enthusiastic, professional, positive and sincere person. These things will come across from the word go, if you follow the basic rules of giving a firm handshake, a friendly smile and maintaining good eye contact throughout the interview. Never lie in the interview or attempt to blag your way through difficult questions. Good preparation should ensure that you don't have to resort to this. Speak clearly and respectfully. Swearing and flirting are definite no-nos.

✓ Practise 'image management'. It is important to look good and to sound professional in an interview. You should feel comfortable in what you wear, but it is better to turn up 'too smart' than 'too casual'. People will take you seriously if you dress respectably. If you are applying for jobs in media or the arts, a suit may not be necessary, but dressing smartly will always give the impression that you care about getting this job.

TOP TIP

It's always a good idea to take some anti-perspirant with you to an interview, as when people are nervous they tend to sweat. You may also find yourself a bit hot and dishevelled if you had to rush to get to the interview in good time (although if you have prepared your journey well, this shouldn't happen!). Make sure you have time to freshen up before the interview. This will help your confidence and spare the interviewers a sweaty handshake or, worse still, a bad odour when you enter the room. On the other hand, don't go overboard on the perfume or aftershave – that would count as a bad odour, too.

✓ Wherever possible, back up your responses to questions with evidence-based replies. For example, if an interviewer asks you how you manage conflict within a team, give a brief general response and then focus on a specific example of how you have done this in the past. Illustrating your answers with real examples gives you the opportunity to focus on your personal contribution and will be more impressive than giving a vague, hypothetical reply.

TOP TIP

Remember that the interview is a two-way process – not only is the organization trying to decide on the best person for the job, you are also trying to decide on the best organization to work for and the best job and career choice for you.

Common mistakes

X You misread the culture or the personality of the person interviewing you

People tend to underestimate the level of formality and professionalism required in an interview. Some interviewers even create a more social than professional situation to catch you off-guard. If you find yourself in an interview with a more casual approach than is appropriate, change your behaviour as soon as you notice. The interviewers are more likely to remember your behaviour at the end of the interview than at the beginning. On the other hand, if the environment or the interviewer is more formal than you realized, don't worry. You are expected to look and act in a highly professional and formal way in an interview. Use your instincts to judge how much you need to change your behaviour to show that you would fit into the company culture.

✗ You use humour inappropriately

To make a situation less tense, people sometimes use humour to lighten the mood. But if you have said something you think is funny and received a negative reaction, it's best not to call attention to the situation by apologizing. Try to act as if nothing happened and go back to behaving professionally. Whatever you do, don't follow inappropriate humour with more humour.

✗ You didn't do your homework

You get to the interview and realize that you really know nothing about this organization. What do you do? Well, hopefully, you arrived early and have some time in reception. Take the opportunity to do some research on your phone. Often, booklets and leaflets found in receptions provide quite a bit of information about the company, its industry, its products and services. Look at them, look around and learn everything you can. Talk to the receptionist and ask them questions that may be helpful to you in the interview. It is possible to learn quite a bit about the organization on the fly, but nothing works better than doing your homework.

✗ You criticize your current or former employer

Avoid this at all costs. It gives the interview a very negative feeling and will leave the interviewer wondering if you would criticize this organization when you left. This kind of criticism usually happens when someone is asked why they are leaving (or have left) their last position. The best way to answer this is to talk about the future rather than the past, and to show your keenness to take on challenging career opportunities.

BUSINESS ESSENTIALS

✓ Be completely familiar with everything on your CV and be prepared to answer any difficult questions on your education and/or work history.

✓ Do your homework on the company before you go for your interview.

✓ Fix your key skills and strengths in your mind, so that you can make sure you mention them when given appropriate opportunities.

✓ Prepare honest and clear answers to standard interview questions.

✓ Remember that you are also interviewing the organization, so have a list of questions for the interviewer ready.

✓ Ask a friend or family member to role-play the interview with you and ask for their feedback.

✓ Arrive early at the interview to give yourself time to relax, freshen up, absorb the atmosphere and even spend time visualizing a successful result.

✓ Be enthusiastic in the interview and excited about the job.

✓ Don't talk about benefits and salary in a first interview, unless the interviewer brings them up.

✓ If you feel you have misread the level of formality required, change your behaviour appropriately as soon as you notice.

> ✔ If you use humour inappropriately, act as if nothing has happened and get back on track. Don't make another joke to cover it up!
>
> ✔ Don't ever criticize your current or former employer. Talk about the future instead.

If you prepare well for an interview by knowing your CV, listing likely questions and responses, researching the company and the people, role-playing the interview and dressing appropriately, you will arrive at the interview feeling confident and enthusiastic. This confidence will help you make the best impression that you can so you may come away feeling proud of yourself for having done your very best – whatever the outcome.

2
Answering tricky interview questions

Job interviews are the single most important part of the work selection process – for you and for your future employer. Once your CV has shown that you meet the basic skills and background requirements, the interview then establishes how well you might fit into an organization's culture and future plans.

Most interview questions are generally straightforward, unambiguous enquiries, but some interviewers like to surprise you by asking questions specifically intended to explore your thinking and expectations. Or they might try to throw you off-guard to see how you react in high-stress or confusing circumstances. Or they may not be intentionally tricky at all. The interviewer may not be very experienced and so ask you questions that seem unrelated to you and the position. Don't let this throw you!

Answering tricky questions successfully could help you gain the position you are applying for, but remember that the nature of the questions, and how your answers are received, can tell you volumes about whether this is a company you would actually want to work for.

Step one:
Prepare for the interview

1. Think about the potential questions
    ✔ Spend time in advance thinking about questions you might be asked during the interview. (In addition to those below, see also the list of eight question topics on pp. 24–25.) Also, study lists of questions that are available online and formulate possible answers. Although you may not be asked those questions specifically, being well prepared will help you feel relaxed, confident and capable – exactly the type of person the interviewer is looking for!

- What specific skills and knowledge can you bring to this job?

- What are your strengths and how can you make sure those are discussed in the interview?

- What are your weaknesses? Do you feel especially worried about discussing them?

- Can you formulate answers to questions about your weaknesses in advance?

- How can you use the interview to learn about the potential employer?

2. Think about the purpose
The best job interviews are positive encounters that allow a two-way exchange of information. It may feel as though the employer has all the power as it is they

who will decide whether or not to offer you the job. But, in fact, it is you who holds the power – it is you who will decide whether or not to accept the job. So interviews are just as important for you as they are for the interviewer. Keeping this power balance in mind will help you stay calm, dignified and clear-headed.

3. Think about the interviewer
It is safe to assume that the interviewer is slightly uncomfortable with the process too. Not many people enjoy grilling a stranger.

✔ Remember that you may be the 25th candidate this week and the interviewer may be quite sick of asking the same old questions and hearing the same rehearsed answers. Remember, too, that the interviewer was once sitting in your seat, applying for his or her job within the company and worrying about the same surprise questions.

Establishing some empathy with the interviewer can help to make the encounter more relaxed.

Step two:
Communicate effectively during the interview

✔ Never lie. Many interviewers do this work for a living, so they have heard all the 'correct' answers many times before. Don't trot out what you think the interviewer wants to hear. Instead, be candid and clear, and use lengthy answers only when you think that demonstrating your thought processes in detail will add valuable information.

✔ Be sure you understand the question. If the question is unclear, ask for clarification. 'I'm not sure what you mean. Could you explain?' or 'Could you rephrase that question?' are perfectly acceptable queries in any civilized conversation. Job interviews are no different. Similarly, if you didn't hear the question properly, don't be afraid to ask for it to be repeated.

✔ Be prepared to answer questions about salary. You can politely decline to give details about past salary and future expectations if you wish, but be warned that this is difficult to do without creating a bad atmosphere in the interview. The most important thing is to keep the focus on your worth, not your cost.

Many companies offer salaries only at a certain percentage above a candidate's previous salary. However, if your previous salary was below the market average or your worth, this doesn't mean you should be forced to accept a lower salary in the future. Decide before you go into the interview of time on a salary range that is acceptable to you. Make sure the top of the range is well above the figure you would be thrilled to accept and the bottom of the range slightly above your predetermined 'walk-away' figure. There is more advice on negotiating your salary in Chapter 14.

Step three:
Deal with tricky questions

There are roughly eight areas of questioning that could pose a challenge in the interview:

● your experience and management skills;

- your opinion about industry or professional trends;

- the reasons why you are leaving your current job;

- the financial or other value of your past work and achievements;

- your work habits;

- your salary expectations;

- your expectations for the future;

- your personality and relationship skills or problems.

TOP TIP

You may be faced with an interviewer who doesn't seem to know why certain questions are being asked – they may be from an outside employment agency. In this case, try to help them, and yourself, by exploring the reasons why the question might be included and what exactly is being looked for in the way of response. This will show that you are not easily rattled and that you can work calmly and co-operatively towards a solution.

✓ Identify the topic areas that might be the trickiest for you, then think carefully about how you might answer them. You don't want to have to try to blag your way through difficult parts of the interview, and you certainly shouldn't lie. However, you should also be wary of rehearsing answers to anticipated questions word for word, as this is likely to come across as false and insincere, too.

✓ Your solutions to 'scenario' type problems will tell the interviewer a lot about you – whether you can make tough decisions, for example, or if you have leadership qualities. Try to answer these kinds of questions based on business strategy.

✓ Questions about your weaknesses are usually designed to discover the extent of your self-knowledge. Keep your answers short and dignified. Identify only one area of weakness that you're aware of, and describe what you are doing to strengthen that area to demonstrate your enthusiasm for self-development. Try to avoid using the response of being a 'perfectionist' as it is a cliché.

Remember, no one is perfect.

TOP TIP

When you are talking about past experiences and giving examples of your work, don't use 'we' and say 'we did this' or 'we did that'. Use the first person: 'I'. This will reflect better upon you even when you are talking about weaknesses, as it demonstrates self-knowledge and the confidence to take responsibility for the decisions you've made.

Common mistakes

✗ You criticize your former employer or colleagues

If you are asked why you are seeking new employment, focus on your positive ambitions, not any past resentments or grudges. Talk about what has worked in your career, not what has failed.

✗ You get angry or defensive

Some questions may be designed to find out how you perform under pressure or react to provocation. Use your social skills to smooth over any uncomfortable moments and try not to bristle at questions you find offensive. And don't take anything personally.

✗ You think interviews are one-sided

Remember, you are at the interview to find out how desirable the job is to you, just as much as to sell your own desirability to the company. This thought will help you to keep your dignity and prevent you from feeling you must answer inappropriate, irrelevant or intrusive questions.

✗ You use scripted answers to anticipated questions

Scripted answers are artificial, and the interviewer has heard them all before. Original responses, even if they are slightly clumsy, will be more valuable both to you and the interviewer. They are a more accurate guide as to whether there is indeed a match between you and your potential new employer.

BUSINESS ESSENTIALS

✓ Don't be thrown by tricky interview questions – be prepared instead.

✓ Spend time in advance thinking about questions you might be asked, and prepare rough answers.

✓ Remember that you are also there to find out about the company and whether you would like to work for them in this job.

✓ Empathize with the interviewer.

✓ Be honest and clear in your answers.

✓ Be sure you understand the questions – if not, ask for clarification.

✓ If asked about your weaknesses, focus on one area and explain how you plan to develop.

✓ Decide ahead of time on a salary range that is acceptable to you.

✓ Remember that you hold some power too. This will help you stay calm and unruffled.

So be prepared for those tricky questions, stay calm and unruffled, and show your potential new employer that you can deal successfully with difficult situations.

3
Handling inappropriate questions in an interview

Occasionally, you may be interviewed by someone who asks inappropriate questions. These may fall into the category of being 'politically incorrect' or may just put you in a difficult position. Even though most interviewers are very professional and well trained in appropriate interviewing techniques, you should still work out a strategy to deal with this situation – just in case.

Step one:
Know when a question is inappropriate

There are two steps in preparing to handle inappropriate questions: 1, deciding what is inappropriate or uncomfortable to you, and 2, deciding how you will respond.

1. Prepare yourself

Think about the issues below as they will help you to be ready to deal with inappropriate questions:

- What kinds of question would feel inappropriate to me?

- If I get asked this kind of question, what does that say about the organization I am applying to?

- How could I deal with inappropriate questions?

2. Find out which interview questions are unlawful

The worst types of inappropriate questions are sometimes unlawful. Legislation has been put in place to ensure employers make their selection decisions based on fair and objective criteria and to assess your suitability for the job, they must avoid asking unfairly discriminatory questions.

This legislation can be extremely complicated, and is often reviewed and modified, but you can find some helpful guidelines at the UK Employment Law website (emplaw.co.uk). Other helpful resources are ACAS, the Advisory, Conciliation and Arbitration Service (acas.org.uk) and the Citizens Advice Bureau (citizensadvice.org.uk).

Very few UK websites will tell you directly which questions are unlawful and which aren't because of the complexity of the issue, but they will inform you about legislation that can help you determine whether you may be being discriminated against in a job interview.

> Legislation in the UK that covers discrimination:
>
> ● the Equal Pay Act;
>
> ● the Sex Discrimination Act;
>
> ● the Equality Act.

Any question that does not relate directly to your ability to do the job may be considered inappropriate. Some of these questions, which also ask about personal circumstances, may be unfairly discriminatory if your answers are taken into account when your potential employer is making the selection of the successful candidate. Examples of such questions in the United Kingdom might be:

a. those which ask about family circumstances. For example:

   ● Are you married, divorced or single?

   ● Are you planning to start a family?

   ● Do you have any children? How old are they?

   ● Will your husband/wife/partner move if we offer you this job?

b. those that refer to your ability to carry out the role with regard to your gender, race, age or sexuality. For example:

   ● How would you feel working for a white female boss?

   ● Why would a woman want a job like this?

- How will you cope with all the travel bearing in mind you're confined to a wheelchair?

- How will you cope with speaking to customers on the phone with English as your second language?

Note that there are some questions about personal circumstances, such as physical ability, previous convictions or religion, that might not necessarily be discriminatory. Before responding, it's important to understand the reasons why you are being asked the question to enable you to target your response in a suitable and professional way.

3. Decide on your boundaries

Make a list of interview questions that would feel inappropriate to you. These might be questions about your personal life or about your partner or children. If you are single, they might be questions about what you enjoy doing after work. It is up to you to decide if the question is inappropriate for you.

4. Think about why the interviewer might be asking this question

Here are some of the possible reasons why an interviewer might ask you what seems to be an inappropriate question:

- ice-breaking: in some instances you might feel that the interviewer is trying to be friendly. In an attempt to ask some nice easy questions to 'break the ice', he or she may, however, have become too personal;

- nerve-calming: if the interviewer can see you are tense and nervous during the interview, he or she may change tack and ask you some questions about your hobbies or likes and dislikes to get you back on to familiar territory;

● bonding: the interviewer might identify with something you have written on your application form or CV, e.g. 'active member of local Christian society' and want to find some common ground;

● poor interviewing technique: you may be being interviewed by someone who is unskilled in the dos and don'ts of interviewing and he or she may not realize the question they are asking is inappropriate;

● deliberate discrimination: in some circumstances, your interviewer may be asking a question designed to assess your suitability for the job based on unlawful or inappropriate criteria.

Step two:
Know how to respond to inappropriate questions

✓ Never let an interviewer intimidate you by asking inappropriate questions. You have a right to be treated professionally and with dignity.

There are different ways you can answer:

● clarification: check you have understood the question, by asking them to clarify what they are asking, 'I'm not sure I understand your question, could you rephrase it for me?' This also gives your interviewer an opportunity to rephrase the question if it was clumsily posed the first time;

- gentle confrontation: this generally means asking the interviewer, 'I'm not sure why you're asking me that. Would you mind explaining the reason behind asking the question so that I can give you a proper answer?';

- compliance: answer the question;

- avoidance: ignore the question and change the subject;

- humour: respond to the question as if it were a joke, giving the interviewer an opportunity to save face and to ask more appropriate questions;

- strong confrontation: tell the interviewer that the question is inappropriate and that you are not going to answer it, but always clarify that you've understood the question and reason behind it first!

TOP TIP

Always keep your cool and give the interviewer the benefit of the doubt before challenging them. If you have misunderstood the question, the embarrassment any kind of confrontation will cause may put you off (not to mention the interviewer) and ruin your chances of success in the rest of the interview.

✔ Decide which response best fits your situation. Consider the factors below when deciding how to respond to any inappropriate questions:

- Why do you think the interviewer is asking the question?

- How intrusive or outrageous is the question?

- Can you see why this question relates to the job you have applied for?

- How strongly do you want the job?

- Is this kind of question a reflection of the corporate culture?

Think about all these factors and decide whether the question seems fairly harmless and can be safely ignored or whether the interviewer's behaviour crosses ethical lines and must be confronted. If you really want the job, you may decide to overlook the question. If the question is so offensive that you know you could never work for this company, you may be more confrontational.

TOP TIP

If you are a woman, a young person or a member of a minority ethnic group there is a greater chance that you may be asked inappropriate questions. UK legislation on this subject can be rather complicated, but it is a good idea to investigate the most common areas where inappropriate questions are asked so that you do not jump to the wrong conclusion or end up being discriminated against. If you are in a position where you feel certain you have been discriminated against during an application, get a second opinion from a lawyer.

Common mistakes

X You want the job so much, you will do anything to please the interviewer and answer a question you feel you shouldn't have been asked

If this happens, you may leave the interview feeling embarrassed, angry or ashamed. To avoid feeling this desperate when you are job-hunting, try to line up several exciting interviews. Also, spend time preparing yourself mentally for the interview, so that you feel a sense of self-worth and self-esteem when you walk into the interview.

X You overreact to the inappropriate question

Some may see every comment as a potential insult and leap to conclusions about why a particular question was asked. The result is that the candidate is unlikely to get the job. If you feel yourself overreacting, remember to check you have done your best to make an accurate assessment of the situation and keep in mind that there are better places to fight your battles – a job interview is probably not the best place to make a point about your political values!

BUSINESS ESSENTIALS

✓ Prepare by thinking about any questions that feel inappropriate or uncomfortable to you and decide how you will respond.

✓ Familiarize yourself with potentially unlawful interview questions and use this knowledge to help you deal with such questions effectively.

✓ Clarify why an interviewer is asking you a particular question if you're unsure of its appropriateness.

✓ Remember, there might be times when you feel that the interviewer is just trying to be friendly and that a short answer is appropriate.

✓ Remember you can choose how to respond to an inappropriate question: humour, clarification, avoidance, compliance, gentle or strong confrontation. Decide which response best fits your situation.

✓ Try not to overreact to inappropriate questions. Save your battles for another time and place.

✓ Avoid feeling desperate when you are job-hunting. Line up other interviews and retain a sense of self-worth and self-esteem.

✓ If you find any of the interview questions really insulting, think hard about whether you really want to work for this company after all.

Remember that you are not forced to answer any questions in an interview that make you feel uncomfortable. Be prepared: decide in advance what you feel would be an inappropriate question and have a possible response ready. This will help prevent you from overreacting and adding to an already tense situation, and give you the confidence to make the best of an interview that might otherwise be going well.

4
Succeeding with application forms

Recruiters frequently employ application forms as an additional 'screening' process when they advertise vacancies. Any application form can be off-putting at first, but below are some tips to help you through.

BUSINESS ESSENTIALS

✓ Read all the questions thoroughly. They're there for a good reason and have been worded very carefully. Think about what the recruiters want to find out about you and give them enough information to do so.

✓ Look carefully at the space provided for 'open' questions (i.e. those that can't be answered by 'yes' or 'no'). How much detail are you expected to go into?

✓ If possible, download the application form so that you can draft some answers. Remember to keep them brief but informative (if not much space is allowed, it's probably deliberate: employers will want to see that you can write concisely).

✓ Don't panic if the computer crashes when you're mid-form. You'll have created a password when you first registered on the site, so should be able to access what you've done so far if you log back in.

✓ Do the questions yourself. You may be tempted to ask some friends to help while you're filling in the answers, but they won't be able to come with you if you're invited to interview!

✓ Only give information you can back up: don't inflate your job title, salary, degree class, you name it. If you're offered the job and are asked to send in the relevant paperwork to prove your claims, what will you do then?

✓ Remember that your writing should be as professional and grammatical as possible; don't lapse into email habits when filling them in: write full sentences, check your spelling and make sure your answers make sense before you submit!

✓ If you are visually impaired, contact the organization in question and let them know so that they can make arrangements to help you. If they won't and are inflexible, they probably wouldn't be an ideal employer anyway.

5
Succeeding in telephone or video interviews

Initial interviews by telephone or video call are relatively common, but they are quite challenging for both parties. You probably normally use the phone, Skype or Zoom to talk with friends whom you know, or for business calls with people you don't need to know personally. Getting to know someone remotely can be awkward. As always, preparation and practice will provide you with some help.

> **BUSINESS ESSENTIALS**
>
> 1. Be well equipped
>
> ✓ Have everything ready before you start: papers, pen, information you will need to put across accurately, dates and so on.
>
> ✓ Make sure your phone/laptop are charged and, for a video call, that your laptop is set at the right height and with adequate lighting.

✓ Think carefully about the likely shape of the interview. What information do you need to give? What questions do you need to ask?

✓ Make sure you find a quiet room for the interview, where you won't be interrupted or have any distractions. You may need to refer to some notes, but try not to rustle your papers too much.

2. On a telephone call:

✓ Be aware of your own voice. Watch the tendency to talk too much! Pauses – even very short ones – are awkward on the phone and with no visual cues to guide you it is tempting to fill spaces with words.

✓ Take care not to become monotonous – your voice is important because you cannot make an impression visually. As in any interview, sound positive, friendly and business-like.

✓ Listen to the interviewer: since you get no visual information on the phone, you should pay careful attention to the non-verbal aspects of speech – tone, pitch, inflection, for example – to pick up clues about what the interviewer is interested in.

✓ Make notes of important facts and agreements – it is easy to forget things when there is no 'picture' to reinforce them.

3. On a video call:

✓ Be sure to look into the camera, not at the screen, especially when speaking. This means that the interviewer will see you looking at them, not away from them. Practise (and record yourself) before the call if this is difficult for you.

✓ Turn off all notifications so that they don't irritate you or the interviewer during the call.

✓ Check that your sound is clear and audible. Again, record yourself before the call if necessary and remove any irritating hiss or crackle (e.g. some computer fans can cause background noise).

✓ Take the call somewhere you won't be interrupted.

✓ If your background is untidy or distracting, use one of the software's filters to blur it out. Be sure to sit still if you do this because otherwise you may disappear from view!

6
Succeeding in competence-based interviews

The idea behind competence-based interviews (often called behavioural interviews) is to determine how well suited you are to a job based upon what you have learnt from situations in the past. Most interviews incorporate some competence-based questions, because research shows that they seem to be the most effective form of assessment, as your knowledge and experience are being judged against the specific criteria of the job.

Competence-based questions usually start with something like 'Give me an example of when . . .' or 'Describe a situation where . . .'

BUSINESS ESSENTIALS

1. Prepare examples

✓ Given that the interview will focus on past experience, it's useful to think about examples you could use to show how you have developed the core competences outlined in the Top Tip on the following page.

✓ When you look back at these experiences, ask yourself the following questions:

- What did I do personally?

- How did I manage to overcome barriers or pitfalls?

- What did I achieve?

- Is there anything I would have or should have done differently?

- What did I learn from the experience?

You may not be asked precisely these questions, but they will prepare you for areas of questioning you are highly likely to encounter in the interview.

2. Know the job

✓ Read the job description very carefully before your interview and focus on the specific requirements of the post. Think about the issues and responsibilities related to the job. You can try to anticipate the sorts of questions you may be asked based on those requirements and responsibilities.

✓ Also think about your present job and in particular how your role fits within the team. Try to identify the transferable skills that you'd be able to carry across into the new job.

TOP TIP

As a rule of thumb, there are certain competences that almost all employers will be interested in. A shortlist of favourites would include: planning and organizing; project management; decision-making; communicating; influencing others; teamwork; achieving results; leadership.

7
Succeeding in internal interviews

Some companies like to use an interview process for filling internal vacancies or making career plans. Within an organization there can be all sorts of assumptions that may complicate this process. For example, some people feel that the company should know them well enough from experience and appraisals to make an interview unnecessary. Others worry about the politics of the situation and the consequences of failure. Some people may be tempted to treat the interview process too informally or lightly, especially if they know their interviewer.

BUSINESS ESSENTIALS

✓ Do your homework and find out as much as you can about the position before taking your application any further. If you have a human resources department, they will probably be the best source of information.

✓ If your interview is for a job in a different department, talk to your boss about your intended move. It could create a very nasty atmosphere if they find out from someone else.

✓ Find out what is required from you, what you can assume the interviewer knows already and how the decision-making process works.

✓ Anticipate what the interviewer will want to know about your experience and competence. Don't take too much for granted in this area.

TOP TIP

As a general rule, treat these interviews as you would an external application until you have definitive information that things are different. It's best to err on the side of formality until you are sure what is required.

8
Succeeding in stress interviews

In stress interviews, candidates are deliberately put under pressure to see how they respond to difficult people or unexpected events. Organizations should use this technique only when they can clearly show the need for it, and even then they should be careful how it is handled, taking account of the sensitivities of the interviewee.

It can be an unnerving experience, but being aware that this is a recognized interviewing technique for some firms will help you to cope should you come across it. The sorts of industries that may employ this technique include banking and some security firms. Stress questions often come in the form of a role play, when the interviewer, in his or her role, may challenge you by saying something like: 'I think your answer is totally inadequate: can't you do better than that?' The interviewer is testing your ability to manage surprises, ambiguity and a confrontational situation. He or she will want to see you keep the initiative, maintain your composure and deal with the situation appropriately.

BUSINESS ESSENTIALS

✔ The trick is not to take the remarks personally but to recognize that you are required to play a role. Take a deep breath, pause, keep your temper and respond as naturally and accurately as you can.

✔ Keep your wits about you because this technique is designed to catch you off-guard. Create time for yourself to balance logic and emotion calmly in framing your response.

✔ Try to anticipate what the next problem will be and keep ahead of the game.

9
Succeeding in assessment centres

This method of selection usually involves a group of candidates performing a number of different tasks and exercises over the course of one to three days. Assessment centres were traditionally used at the second stage of recruitment, but nowadays it is not uncommon to be asked to one at the first stage.

Assessment centres usually include:

1. Group exercises: role-playing, discussion, leadership exercises

2. Individual exercises. For example:

   - written tests (such as report-writing based on case studies);

   - in-tray exercises (a business simulation where you are expected to sort through an in-tray, making decisions about how to deal with each item) presentation of an argument or data analysis;

- psychometric tests (please see Chapter 13 for more information);

- interviews.

3. Social events

4. Company presentations

You will be assessed most of the time – the administrator should clarify this for you – so there's rarely an opportunity to let down your guard.

BUSINESS ESSENTIALS

Being called to an assessment centre can be a nerve-racking experience. However, you can make these events a little less stressful by following a few simple rules.

✓ The organization will probably tell you what they are looking for in their career literature or their invitation. Make sure you have read this, thought about it and worked out how you can show the behaviours they are interested in.

✓ Behave naturally but thoughtfully. Do not attempt to play an exaggerated role – it is never what the assessors want to see! Unnatural behaviour quickly becomes inappropriate and boorish.

✓ Make sure that you take part fully in all activities; assessors can only appraise what you show them.

✓ Don't be over-competitive. The assessors are likely to be working to professional standards, not looking for the 'winner'.

✔ Take an overview. Most of the exercises have a purpose wider than the obvious. Try to stand back and look at things in context rather than rushing straight in. With the in-tray exercise, for example, you will probably find that some items are related and need to be tackled together.

10
Succeeding in technical interviews

In technical interviews, candidates are asked specific questions relating to technical knowledge and skills. As you'd imagine, they are common in research and technology companies' selection processes. The organization will normally tell you in advance that they hold a technical interview or if they want you to give a presentation on your thesis or experience. You need to be prepared for 'applied' questions that ask for knowledge in a different form from the way you learned it at college.

For example, 'How would you design a commercially viable wind turbine?' or 'How would you implement the requirements of data-protection legislation in a small international organization?'

BUSINESS ESSENTIALS

✔ Consider the 'audience' and how your knowledge fits with their likely interests and priorities. What questions are they likely to ask?

✔ Sometimes these presentations go wrong when interviewers ask very 'obvious' questions; or one of them has a favourite or 'trick' question. It is easy to be irritated by these, but you should remain calm and courteous. Try to see the interviewers as your 'customer' and respond with patience.

✔ As always, preparation and anticipation are the keys to success. Work out what your interviewers will want to know and make sure your knowledge is up to scratch in the correct areas.

11
Succeeding in panel interviews

When you are looking for a job, sooner or later you may be asked to attend a panel interview. These interviews are becoming increasingly popular in private and public sectors as they:

- save time and are efficient. Several interviewers meet in one place at one time, so the applicant does not need to be shuffled around from office to office. In addition, as there is no schedule to follow, there is no danger of over-running;

- provide consistent information. You, as the job applicant, only need to tell your story once to the panel. This saves you having to repeat it over and over again in private meetings with interviewers.

Although it can be quite intimidating to walk into an interview where several people are present, a panel interview is also an excellent opportunity for you to show your strengths to a number of interviewers all at once.

A successful panel interview is one in which you come across as composed and confident – and able to handle whatever is thrown your way.

BUSINESS ESSENTIALS

1. Do your homework

✓ As with any job interview, find out about the organization as well as the position you are applying for. Start with the company website, if it has one, and try to get a copy of its annual report. Look at their social media feeds and talk to people who are familiar with the organization. You are trying to get a feel for its key values, success factors and people.

2. Prepare mentally for the possibility of a panel interview

✓ Consider the points below before going to any job interview:

-   How can I prepare myself mentally for a panel interview?

-   What are my major selling points?

-   How can I get these across to each member of the panel?

✓ Try 'visualization'. This is a very good way of helping you feel and appear relaxed and confident. Before your interview, imagine what a panel interview might be like. Visualize yourself in a conference room with several people sitting around a large table. Imagine answering each question easily, bonding with each interviewer and having a successful interview.

Some people are uncomfortable using the visualization technique, but it is a very effective method. The retired golfer Jack Nicklaus claims that much of his success came from mentally rehearsing each shot before he actually picked up a club. What has worked so well for him can work for you, too.

3. Answer the questions

✓ Sometimes in a panel interview it can feel as though questions are coming at you from all directions. Try to take the first question, answer it, then build on that answer to respond to the second interviewer. Make sure you answer every question. You do not want one of the interviewers thinking that you ignored his or her question.

✓ Clarify questions if necessary. If you find a question confusing, don't be afraid to ask for further explanation. Phrases such as, 'Just to clarify . . .' or, 'If I understand correctly, you want to know . . .' can help you understand exactly what information the interviewers are looking for.

✓ As you are talking, make eye contact with each member of the panel in turn. This means catching the gaze of a particular member of the panel, holding it for about three seconds, and then moving to the next panel member. In reality, it is very difficult to look someone in the eye, count to three, and then move on, all while answering a challenging question. However, this is a very useful skill to use in meetings and public speaking, and will become second nature after a bit of practice.

✓ Resist the temptation to take the less pressurized route by letting members of the panel do all the talking. Remember, you are selling yourself, and to do that you need to get your point across. If the people on the panel do all the talking, all they will remember about you is that you may be a good listener. Of course, you should certainly not interrupt members of the panel, but do make sure you discuss your strengths and the reasons they should employ you. Sell yourself as you would in a one-to-one interview.

TOP TIP

If you are unsure, check that your answers were understood and that you have answered the question fully. Simply ask the appropriate person, 'Did I answer your question?'

12
Succeeding in 'hypothetical' or scenario-based interviews

Most interviewers have been carefully trained to look only for evidence and facts from the candidate's past and therefore never to ask hypothetical questions. But sometimes – and especially with younger candidates who don't have much past work experience – an organization will be more interested in what the person can become in the future rather than what they are capable of now.

There are techniques for doing this. They normally focus on exploring how you think and act when confronted with problems you haven't experienced before – rather than what you think and do. The logic is that in order to learn from a new experience you must be able to understand the experience thoroughly. These interviews assess the level of complexity at which you can think – and therefore understand the issues and learn how to deal with them.

Typically, you'll be asked in these interviews to take part in a conversation that gets more complex and wide-ranging as it progresses. You build a scenario further and further into the future. There are no 'right' answers, of course: the interviewer is looking for an ability to spot the right questions.

Knowing that the interview will take this form is some help, but there is really little that you can do to prepare for it. Being well rested and alert, relaxing and enjoying the challenge are the best tips.

13
Understanding psychometric tests

Large organizations often use tests as a way of working out whether or not a candidate has the knowledge, skills and personality needed for a particular job. These are called psychometric tests. They can help identify those people who may be suitable for future leadership positions. Psychometric tests are also often used to help in career guidance and counselling.

Step one:
Prepare for the test

✓ Find out about the different types of psychometric test and think about the following to help you prepare:

- How should I prepare for the different types of psychometric test?

- Are there resources that can help me prepare for a particular kind of test?

- Are there test-taking skills that I can learn?

- What can I do if I don't like the results of the test?

✔ Be physically prepared for taking a psychometric test. Research has shown that people perform better in all kinds of psychometric tests when they are well rested and in good physical shape. And, strangely, people do better in tests when they are slightly hungry, so eat lightly before taking one! Also, make sure you have some water with you. Dehydration may affect your concentration.

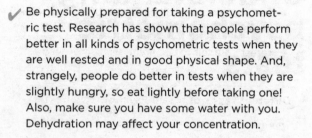

TOP TIP

If you are just beginning your career, or if you are thinking about a major career change, psychometric testing can help you work out which careers would best fit your interests, skills and personality. (If you are about to leave university, talk to your career development officers about the range of tests they can provide.)

1. Attainment and aptitude tests

These tests have 'right answers', so you can improve your score with practice.

✔ Before you go for the test, find out exactly what skills and knowledge are being tested. It is a really good idea to practise the kind of test you are taking and there are hundreds of test preparation websites and books available. These explain how the questions are structured, provide test-taking tips and contain sample tests so that you can evaluate your own level of skills and knowledge. It's best to:

● take a sample test;

● use study guides to help strengthen your weaker areas;

● retest yourself to see if you have improved.

Different types of test 1: Psychometric tests

There are three main types:

1. Attainment tests. These are tests designed to find out how much you have learnt from your past training and experience – much like school exams. If you are applying for your first real job you might be confronted with a test of maths, English or IT skills, for example.

2. General intelligence tests. This group and the next are concerned with your ability to learn new skills. Intelligence tests measure your capacity for abstract thinking and reasoning in particular contexts. The items usually cover numerical, verbal and symbolic reasoning, often in the familiar forms, such as: 'What is the missing number in this series . . .?'

3. Special aptitude tests. Some types of work clearly require you to have – or be able to learn – particular skills at a high level. This group of tests is designed to reveal general or specific aptitudes that the employer needs to develop. The most usual types of test are:

- verbal ability: including verbal comprehension, usage and critical evaluation;

- numerical ability: involving numerical reasoning or analysis of quantitative data;

- spatial ability: relating to skill at visualizing and manipulating three-dimensional shapes, for example;

- analytical reasoning: relating to the way in which candidates can read and process complex arguments. These tests are very common among graduates and those applying for MBAs;

- IT aptitude: various tests for technical programming ability and word processing;

- Manual dexterity: testing special manipulation or hand-eye co-ordination linked to the special requirements of a job. If you are applying for a modern apprenticeship, especially in engineering or technology, you may meet these.

2. Personality and interest tests

Since these tests measure your interests, personal preferences and your ability to learn new skills, you can't really prepare for these tests in the same way that you would for a maths or history exam. Career-related aptitude tests are based on self-awareness, so the more you know yourself, the more likely the test results are to be useful to you.

✔ Spend time thinking about your life and career goals, and the things you most like to do.

TOP TIP

Look up the Strong Interest Inventory® (sometimes known as the Strong-Campbell Interest Inventory® or SCII). This is a widely used and popular career test that suggests career choices based on the interests of the person being tested.

✓ Be well rested and relaxed so that you can focus clearly on the questions and provide your best answers.

✓ Find copies of the test that will be used, or a similar one. Familiarity with the style of the test will give you confidence.

Different types of test 2: Psychometric 'inventories'

There are four types in general use:

1. Personality questionnaires. The use of these instruments is very widespread and this is the type of test you are most likely to meet, especially if you are a graduate. The tests are designed to measure particular personality traits or characteristics that are important in general or specific work contexts. Examples are motivation, sociability, resilience and emotional adjustment.

    Most of these inventories are 'self-report': they ask you to say how you would respond to a variety of situations by choosing from a list of possibilities. You may find that they ask very similar questions several times over to judge the fine detail of your responses, and in many cases to check that you are answering straightforwardly and not trying to create a particular impression! The majority of the inventories you will come across compare your responses with those of other people like you, or groups of people who are successful in the type of work you are applying for. These are called normative tests. A few will measure the relative strengths of different traits within your make-up, independent of other people. This type is called *ipsative*.

2. Interest inventories. These questionnaires are designed to find out where your career interests lie and the areas of work at which you are likely to be most successful. You will find them being used for career guidance in any careers service office, in some selection processes and for later development of people within an organization.

3. Values questionnaires. Values, motives or life goals guide your choices and are very important in determining the types of work and work contexts in which you are most likely to succeed. These questionnaires explore collections of values that are relevant to the workplace, such as the need for achievement, order and belonging.

4. Others. One or two more specialized tests that might be met include:

   ● sales aptitude: various tests concerned with the special skills and attitudes needed for selling are in use;

- leadership: while most of the personality inventories will have a leadership dimension, there are some specialized tests that focus on leadership behaviours such as planning, communication and implementing ability;

- alternative methods: though not widely accepted in the UK, many European employers use graphology as a means of appraising personal characteristics. If you are asked to hand-write your application letter, this is probably being used.

TOP TIP

Look online for practice tests: there are lots of free examples of most of the widely used tests and plenty of information about how they are used. Some sites are listed at the end of the book.

Step two:
Learn test-taking skills

✔ Read the instructions very carefully. Make sure you understand them completely. Don't be afraid to ask for clarification from the person administering the test.

Many people dive right into the test and so get a much lower score than they deserve because they missed some important information.

For example, in some tests, unanswered questions do not count against you. The instructions may tell you that wrong answers will be subtracted from right answers to provide a final score for the test. In this case, you should skip over questions for which you're not sure of the answer – don't just guess. Some tests are timed and, if so, it's important to know how much time you have left so you can focus on the questions that you are most likely to answer correctly.

✓ When taking a 'personality' test, it is usually a mistake to spend too long pondering your responses. Generally speaking, the response that comes immediately to mind will be the best one.

A good test-taking strategy

✓ First go through the whole test, answering only the questions you are sure of.

✓ Go back over the unanswered questions and tackle the ones that you are confident about.

✓ If you still have time left, go through the remaining questions once again, really think them through and then provide your best answer.

Remember that different companies will administer tests in different ways. You may find yourself taking the test remotely, or at a venue on your own or in a roomful of other people. However, not everyone at the venue will necessarily be applying for the same job as you; some companies may hold 'testing days' in which they test all applicants for all vacancies at the same time.

Step three:
Reflect on the results

✓ If you are taking a test for career guidance, take the results as an indicator – extra information to add to what you already know about yourself. Think carefully about the results but remember that no test is completely accurate and no one knows you better than you do yourself. If the career advice provided by the test seems too far off the mark, trust your intuition. You may want to take a different kind of career test as a second opinion.

TOP TIP

If you are taking tests for career-planning purposes, take several different tests, compare the results and look for themes and patterns.

If you are taking an attainment or aptitude test as part of a job application, the organization should give you an indication of how you did, even if they don't give you more detailed results. For some companies, that indication may be an invitation to interview (if the test took place as an initial screening process), for others, an invitation to a second interview (if the test took place as part of your initial interview). In any case, you have the right to ask for feedback if you have any questions about the whole process. In most organizations, a lot of effort has been made to make sure the tests measure what they're supposed to. If you are in any doubt ask for an explanation of how the test results are used and what the organization has done to see that they are fair to all applicants.

✔ It is usually the human resources department of a company that is responsible for the tests, so if you have questions about your results, and they have a human resources department, contact them first.

Common mistakes

✗ You decide to make a major career shift based on your test results

Test results are meant to be used for guidance and should only be part of a comprehensive career-planning process. This process should include self-assessment exercises, plenty of personal soul-searching, talking to trusted friends and family, and possibly chatting things through with a professional career coach.

✗ You don't take the test seriously

Your CV looks good, you know some people in the organization and you have a lot of confidence in your ability to charm the recruitment manager – so you don't give much thought to the test you are asked to take. However, even though the results can be taken with a pinch of salt, you should adopt a serious attitude towards taking the test. Organizations that use testing often use the results at the very beginning of the recruitment process. If you don't pass the test, you will not even be considered for an interview. If there is a test, be as prepared as possible to do it and to do it well.

✗ You take the test too seriously

Many people get excessively concerned about psychometric tests, but the fact is that they can have such a varied predictive validity that some are only slightly better than chance. Don't feel you've failed if tests don't go to plan, and remember that the company is measuring itself as well as you.

✗ You stay up all night the night before, cramming for the test

This, and a lot of caffeine, may have been how you got yourself through tests and exams before, so perhaps it has become the way you tackle all tests. But it wasn't a good strategy then, and it's not a good strategy now. The students who did best in final exams were those who began preparing right at the beginning of term – slow and steady wins the race. So if you know you will be taking a psychometric test, find out as much as you can about the test and study over a period of time on a regular basis. If you have to take a 'personality test' there is little you can do to prepare, so don't worry about it!

BUSINESS ESSENTIALS

✔ Before an aptitude or interest test, spend time thinking about your life and career goals, and the things you enjoy doing.

✔ The two most common aptitude tests measure verbal reasoning and mathematical ability. These tests can also predict your likely academic success and how you might perform in certain job situations.

✔ You will perform better in psychometric tests if you are well rested, in good physical shape – and slightly hungry!

✔ Before you take an aptitude test, find out exactly what skills and knowledge are being tested. Use a test preparation booklet and practise, or at least become familiar with, the test style.

✔ When taking the test, read the instructions very carefully and ask for clarification if you don't understand something.

✔ A good method for test-taking is to go through the whole test a number of times, answering only the questions you are sure of first.

✔ Remember to take test results as just one indicator, and trust your intuition if the results seem off the mark.

✔ Adopt a serious attitude towards taking any test: it may be what gets you an interview.

Whatever you think of psychometric tests, they are an increasingly important part of the job-hunting process. Find out what tests you might be asked to take, get hold of similar tests and practise. That way, you'll feel confident and ready to do your best and, hopefully, come away with a date for an interview in your diary.

14
Negotiating a better package for your new job

If you make it through the tests and convince them of your fantastic worth at interview, a job offer may be just around the corner and you face having to talk about your financial value.

When you are offered a new job, you have a unique opportunity to position yourself as a valuable asset in the organization and to set your level of remuneration accordingly. To achieve this, you need to establish an appropriate asking price – and it is wise to think about this early in case it should come up during your interview. On the one hand, you don't want to oversell yourself and price yourself out of the market. On the other, you need to avoid selling yourself short, as it is extremely difficult to change your position once you're placed in a complex pay structure.

There are no definite rules about how to conduct your negotiation. Every situation differs and each employer has their own set of thresholds. Understanding the context in which your negotiation takes place and sensitivity to the culture of the organization is therefore vital. Having said that, there are some practical steps you can take to position yourself sensibly.

Step one:
Research the employer

When you are going for a job, you are effectively a salesperson promoting a product, and it is up to you to demonstrate that the 'product' is valuable, high-quality and superior to anything a competitor could offer.

✔ Like a salesperson, you need to know your market and your buyers. Potential employers, or 'buyers', will, of course, be looking for the best possible value for their money. However, if you have positioned yourself well and made a good impression at interview, they won't risk losing you and will be prepared to settle at the top of the market rather than the bottom. If you know what the employer can afford, you will automatically gain an advantage.

TOP TIP

Before entering the negotiation, do specific research. This means familiarizing yourself with the company itself, as well as the range of salary and benefit options that are being offered. Don't assume you'll be offered more than your former salary, especially if you're competing with someone who is equally qualified but willing to work for less. If the salary offered is less than you had hoped for, you can discuss the benefits package and make provision for an early salary review.

Step two:
Consult external sources

When seeking an entry point for your salary, there are several sources you can turn to in order to find an appropriate figure for your industry.

✓ Look at the range of packages offered for similar positions.

✓ Ask for advice from people in your professional and personal network.

✓ Ask your mentor, if you have one, to advise you – or use their own network to access the information.

✓ If you are a member of a union, they will have information on acceptable salary ranges for your profession.

✓ Try some of the free salary calculators online.

> **TOP TIP**
>
> You can put off a prospective employer by pitching too high or too low, so it is important to get your level right. Get a feel for the market rate by drawing information from the above sources.

Step three:
Discuss salary as late as possible

It is preferable to leave salary discussions until the point at which you are offered the job. However, it is not always the case that this will be left until the final stages of the process.

✔ Many recruiters ask for salary expectations and details of current salary early in the process. Some even screen people out on this basis. If this is the case, you may need to spend some time researching the question of salary at the application stage or before the first meeting. This will require you to think about your aspirations and to be absolutely sure of the territory you would like to tread, the experience you would like to gain and the context in which you would like to work.

✔ If you are forced to answer a question about your salary hopes at the beginning of the recruitment process, have a figure ready that is at the higher end of the scale. You can always supplement this with a request for a particular benefits package.

Step four:
Consider the whole package

Some employers have fixed-scale salaries, in which case there is little room for negotiation. However, you may find that the total package of pay and benefits raises the worth of the salary to an acceptable level. For instance, you may be offered private health cover, a non-contributory pension, a fully financed car, and bonus potential. Other benefits to consider when negotiating a package would be holiday days, relocation money if you need to move house, childcare facilities, flexible working, the working from home set-up, mobile phones and laptops.

- ✓ When bonuses are mentioned you may want to discuss the basis on which the bonus is paid so that you are absolutely clear of the terms and conditions attached to it. Some bonus schemes spread the payments over several years as an incentive to stay with the business. Such complexities can be very off-putting.

- ✓ Remember the tax implications. All the benefits included in a package are taxed as 'benefits in kind'. Company cars are taxed on the basis of the price when first registered. You may want to consider whether you need a car with a large capacity or whether running a car with a smaller engine could improve your income tax situation. As a result of the rapid depreciation of new cars, many people are now opting for a salary increase instead of a car allowance. Private health insurance is taxed at its cash value. This would make another impact on your tax bill.

- ✓ Many companies are strict about the personal use of equipment such as mobile phones, cars and laptops. Find out about the terms of use in case it turns out your employers are the only ones to benefit from these perks.

Step five:
Explore the boundaries

Adverts sometimes carry salary ranges to give applicants an idea of the boundaries of the negotiation. You can be sure, however, that the negotiation will start at base level.

✔ If you find that the employer is not responding to your sales pitch, you could negotiate an early pay review instead: for instance, if you demonstrate your worth against certain criteria in the first six months of employment, they will agree to a particular salary increase. Ensure that the criteria are clearly set, though, and that they are included in your contract of employment.

✔ Some adverts state that the salary is 'negotiable'. The onus is then on you to move in with an offer. Again, try to leave it to the end of the recruitment process, and be sure that you have studied the equivalent packages for the type of role and industry sector you are applying for.

✔ Some firms are more flexible about benefits than they are about salary. Find out if you can exchange a benefit, such as a car or some holiday days, for a cash equivalent. This will be easier in smaller organizations that don't have inflexible systems in place.

✔ If you are successful in your negotiations, ask for the agreed terms and conditions confirmed in writing before you resign from your current position.

Common mistakes

✗ Not doing your research

It is a common, misguided belief that requesting a high salary will convey a greater sense of your worth. The prospective employer will naturally ask why you think you are worth so much. If you don't have a rational argument, you will look ill-prepared and unprofessional. Time invested in research is always well spent. In this way, you can argue your case professionally and logically.

✗ Bluffing

Don't bluff in your negotiation and try to play off fictitious job offers against the real one you're hoping to get. Employers generally don't respond to this kind of pressure, and instead of receiving a speedy offer you're likely to be left with nothing.

✗ Being too interested in the package

Beware of seeming more interested in the package than in the role you are being recruited for. Every employer knows that you will want a fair deal, but you need to demonstrate that your financial concerns are balanced by a genuine desire for the job.

BUSINESS ESSENTIALS

✓ Research the company before you start negotiations.

✓ Look at the wider industry to help identify your level.

✓ When you start negotiating, make sure you know your minimum acceptable salary – but don't reveal this figure!

✓ Try to avoid discussing the package until you have been offered the position.

✓ If you are asked to name a figure, don't lie, but offer a range within which you would be prepared to negotiate.

✓ Remember to include benefits, bonuses and pay reviews as part of your negotiation.

✓ Get the whole deal in writing before resigning from your current position.

BUSINESS ESSENTIALS

Psychometric tests: Sample questions

Although there are many different types of psychometric test, and many organizations producing them, there is not a great deal of diversity in terms of the kinds of structures used for the questions. For example, you will almost always be confronted with the multiple-choice format. Therefore, it is a good idea to familiarize yourself with the most common question forms found in the most widely used kinds of tests. To start you off, here are some examples that will give you a flavour of the sort of questions you may be asked. You can follow this up with more research.

General intelligence tests

Example 1

Write down the letter printed below the word that should come in the middle, if the following were arranged in a sequence:

Bridge	Soccer	Squash	Sculling	Basketball
P	Q	R	S	T

Example 2

What is the third member of this series?

| 9 | 18 | ?? | 72 | 144 |

Example 3

Complete the equation using one of the sets of shapes.

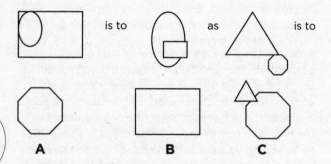

A   **B**   **C**

Special aptitude tests

One of the most common types of question format used in aptitude tests is one where you are presented with some data from which you need to extrapolate facts and/or meaning. In verbal ability tests, this will probably mean answering questions based on a paragraph of text (see Example 1). In a numerical ability test, this may mean answering questions based on graphical or tabular information. Gap-filling activities are also very popular in aptitude tests, as are completing series of words, numbers or shapes (see Example 2).

Verbal ability

Example 1

Below you will see a statement of facts, followed by a number of conclusions that some people might make based on the facts. Examine these conclusions carefully and decide how true each is. Mark each T if it is definitely true; PT if it is probably true, but not conclusively proved; ID if there is insufficient data to decide on its truth; PF if it is probably false; and F if the conclusion is definitely incorrect.

It is quite difficult to grasp the pace of developments in science and technology over the last century. People quickly take innovations for granted and expect things to get better/smarter/faster all the time. It would surprise most people to learn that the lives of Orville Wright – co-inventor of powered flight – and John Glenn the US astronaut, overlapped by more than 20 years.

Conclusions	T	PT	ID	PF	F
Orville Wright and John Glenn were close friends.	☐	☐	☐	☐	☐
Wright was one of the first people to believe that flying is possible.	☐	☐	☐	☐	☐
Glenn was born more than 20 years before Orville Wright died.	☐	☐	☐	☐	☐
Technology changes too quickly for most people.	☐	☐	☐	☐	☐
Most people are surprised to realize how fast aviation technology has progressed.	☐	☐	☐	☐	☐

Example 2

Look at the pairs of words and decide how they are related. Then choose the word that best completes the last pair.

origami   paper
cookery   food
brick-laying   cement
sewing   ?

A   **B**   **C**   **D**

knitting   shirt   needle   hem

Numerical ability

Example 1

Choose the number that should replace the question mark.

26   x   ?   =   57   +   47

Example 2

Your assistant started on £17,000 per year and receives an 8% pay rise. What is their new salary?

A   B   C   D   E

18,280   18,360   18,420   18,440   18,460

Personality questionnaires

These are the least stressful and most fun type of psychometric test to do, as there are no right or wrong answers and you can learn things about yourself. The favoured advice with these is to answer the questions as quickly and honestly as you can.

You should base your responses on how you feel at the time, rather than on how you may have felt in the past or speculation about how you might feel in the future. It is also better to give the response that comes to you naturally – thinking too deeply about how you are going to answer not only takes a lot of time but usually adds little to your immediate response anyway.

It is not worth trying to guess what the test is looking for in order to work out the 'correct' answers.

Most tests have mechanisms for spotting when you are doing this! There will probably be many questions for which you find yourself agreeing with more than one of the answers. This is normal – people are not easily categorized!

Example 1

Choose the statement you are most likely to make.

✓ The vision is more important than the process.

✓ I'm interested in what others have done in similar situations.

✓ You should make a decision and stick to it.

✓ Things should be left open and flexible for as long as possible.

Choose the letter that best describes how you see yourself.

A   Innovative and resourceful in solving complex problems.
B   Empathetic and good in motivating others.
C   Excellent at organizing and deciding procedures.
D   Alert, confident and persuasive in negotiation.

Example 2

For each of the statements below rate yourself on the five-point scale.

strongly agree	agree	unsure	disagree	strongly disagree

I am often influenced by my emotions

| ☐ | ☐ | ☐ | ☐ | ☐ |

'Taking part is more important than winning' is a sensible maxim

| ☐ | ☐ | ☐ | ☐ | ☐ |

I enjoy repairing things

| ☐ | ☐ | ☐ | ☐ | ☐ |

Where to find more help

What Color is Your Parachute? 2021: Your Guide to a Lifetime of Meaningful Work and Career Success

Richard N. Bolles, Berkley Publishing Corporation, 2020

Possibly the only book on careers and job-hunting you need.

nationalcareers.service.gov.uk/

eu.themyersbriggs.com/en/tools/Strong-Interest-Inventory

prospects.ac.uk/careers-advice/interview-tips

reed.co.uk/career-advice/how-to-prepare-for-an-interview/

psychometricinstitute.co.uk/

Index